Islamic Architecture

...y Hutt and
...rd Harrow

Scorpion Publications Limited

First published 1977 by
Scorpion Publications Limited
P.O. Box No 1 London WC2E
ISBN 0 905906 00 4

Managing Editor: Antony Hutt
Series Editor: Leonard Harrow
Design and Art Direction: Colin Larkin
Design Assistant: Rhonda Larkin
Photographic: Antony Hutt, John Warren,
Warwick Ball, and Leonard Harrow
Set in Monophoto Ehrhardt 453 and 573
Printed on Blade Coated Matt Art 081/120 gsm
Originated, filmset, printed and bound by
Westerham Press Ltd Westerham Kent

Contents

Acknowledgements

We would like to acknowledge the assistance of
the British Institute of Persian Studies, Tehran,
the Archaeological Service of the Ministry of Arts
and Culture, Iran, and other friends and
colleagues in obtaining the photographic
material, and also Dr Eleanor Sims for her
perusal of the manuscript.
Unless otherwise stated all the photographs are by
Antony Hutt.

List of Illustrations

Series note

This volume forms part of an extensive series of illustrated works covering most aspects of Islamic art and architecture. While these books will serve as a source of reference for the serious student, they are also intended to provide the general reader with a lucid and up-to-date introduction to the subject.

Transliteration note

For the sake of simplicity the transliteration of
words from the Arabic script has been made
without the use of diacritical marks and macrons.
The original spellings in Arabic script will be
obvious to those in a position to know; for the
general reader the problem is of no importance.

The Greater Iranian World

To Our Parents

Introduction

In any survey of the Islamic world, particularly one which were to take the Mediterranean Arab heartland as its point of departure, the essential difference of Iran and the Iranian world would be most striking. Ethnically, linguistically, historically and even in its religious convictions, Iran differs from most of the Islamic world, a fact well illustrated in the development of architecture in Islamic Iran.

Architecture and calligraphy are generally regarded as the greatest arts of Islam, arts which are often combined. At times it seems that architecture merely provides the surface on which increasingly complicated inscriptions are carved, moulded or variously and colourfully set down. Of the two arts, however, it can be argued that Iran's major contribution lies in architecture. Ideas and forms originating in pre-Islamic Iran were transformed and embellished during the Islamic period to become some of the greatest forms of expression of the Islamic world and an inspiration to the whole eastern part of that world.

The greatest of Iran's Islamic monuments have become increasingly well known in recent years. At times, however, the clue to the development of a particular style or motif lies with less famous monuments. Reference will be made pictorially to the major monuments and where appropriate, trends will be illustrated by some lesser-known buildings.

The concept of Iran used in the title of this work needs to be defined because the modern boundaries within which we have confined ourselves are historically misleading. Present-day Iran lies at the centre of a greater Iranian world which included Transoxiana (the area north of the River Oxus) and the whole of the eastern provinces of Khurasan and Sistan, much of which now lie within the borders of the Soviet Union and Afghanistan. During our period there was great mobility of people; not only did rulers and power continually cross modern boundaries, but tribal migrations, the movements of trade through merchants' caravans, and above all the constant interchange of craftsmen and artists resulted in a movement of ideas, designs and patterns throughout the area. Such local exchanges combined themselves on a global scale in the institution of the yearly pilgrimage to Mecca, the *Hajj*, to give a sense of unity to the Islamic world which in part is dissipated by modern national boundaries.

Iran's position at the heart of a network of trade and cultural exchange routes thus carried the thoughts and ideas of her artists and scholars throughout the Islamic world as they had done in earlier times. Many deeply-held Persian traditions unconsciously influenced the development of Islamic civilisation and the characteristic mysticism of Iran was influential in the emergence of the esoteric movements of Islam, known collectively as Sufism.

Yet with all this great cultural and scholastic energy, no great urban centre of the ancient or indeed the mediaeval Islamic world ever developed in Iran. Conurbations such as Baghdad, Constantinople or Cairo never emerged as natural centres of Iranian culture. Instead different dynasties moved the capital to any number of sites perhaps following an earlier migratory Persian tradition. Thus there has not been the concomitant accumulation of major monuments of all periods within one restricted area, as is the case with Cairo; rather it has meant that almost every major town throughout the country has at one time or another been a political centre; towns in all parts of the country tend to possess fine buildings from particular periods.

Finally with regard to these various points, an historical framework has been adopted which, although somewhat arbitrary, does provide useful signposts. For despite the traditional nomenclature used by art historians with its resultant tidy divisions, architectural development is not often linked to dynastic history. The period's history is very complex, but if it were to be analysed without some sort of historical framework a survey of the extant monuments might be confusing.

To the coming of the Saljuqs (mid-seventh to mid-eleventh centuries)

There are remarkably few Islamic buildings remaining in Iran before the coming of the Saljuqs and about these there is very little information other than what can be gleaned by stylistic analysis. Many of the relevant historical texts refer to particular monuments, but time has often dealt harshly with these; either early monuments have totally disappeared or those extant do not correspond to the descriptions. This has led to much speculation, but unfortunately the extant body of material is insufficient to clarify matters. In a way the situation is similar to that of Saxon monuments in England; indeed the coming of the Normans in 1066 is close in time to the Saljuqs' entry into Iran from about 1040 onwards. In the same way that there is a paucity of Saxon material in England compared with that which remains from the Norman period, so in Iran Saljuq monuments greatly outnumber those of the earlier age.

The advent of the Saljuqs provides a convenient point historically to terminate the period. Iran then comes under one rule: but artistically, and particularly architecturally, there is no dividing line. Indeed the innovations which are normally associated with the Saljuqs can be shown to pre-date their arrival by at least fifty years, coinciding with the arrival of the first Central Asian Turks as rulers of parts of the Iranian world.

The initial conquest of the Persian Empire by the Muslim Arabs in the seventh century took place with breathtaking speed. The empire of the Sasanians which had fought Romans and Byzantines for centuries was annexed by the all-conquering Arabs in a decade and by the death of the last Sasanian emperor, in 652, most of Iran acknowledged Muslim rule. The rule of Islam should not, however, be equated with total conversion to the religion for this was a slow process, considerably hampered by various revolts and the continued effective independence of a number of regions.

Insofar as buildings remain from this early period they seem to fall under the influence of western Islamic styles, an assumption reinforced by archaeological evidence. Only in the late ninth and tenth centuries is there a resurgence of forms which relate to earlier Iranian models. This seems to be coupled with the beginnings of a national self-awareness. Many of the earliest structures were built of perishable materials, such as wood and sun-dried bricks, and have consequently disappeared. Various natural catastrophes such as earthquakes and fire, as well as endemic warfare, were equally destructive factors for buildings. The Saljuq and subsequent periods saw much rebuilding so that few buildings in the main centres have survived unchanged. The Jami' mosque in Isfahan demonstrates this tendency perfectly; indeed only in recent years have tenth-century columns been discovered actually encased within the later Saljuq piers. As an historical document the city of Isfahan is of extreme importance, in that not only has it rarely been sacked, but it lies in an almost earthquake-free zone. Thus it has important architectural remains from each major period.

Naturally mosques and various associated monuments are the most important extant structures. In general, religious buildings throughout the Islamic world have been better built, whereas secular buildings, such as palaces, were regularly rebuilt by successive rulers and in any case were much more ephemeral in concept. Particularly in Iran the idea of a palace followed that of the ancient world, being a series of pavilions in a garden or park area, and had little in common with the later European concept of a single large building containing the entire court structure. Such a form was also alien to the Islamic way of life which has total mobility of occupational space, making no distinction between eating, sleeping and living areas. This complete mobility is applicable to all levels of society; the various distinctions in room construction have climatic rather than utilitarian causes and movement is from winter to summer rooms rather than from eating to sleeping areas.

As with the development of the Christian church which has a longitudinal axis because of its processional requirements, the mosque assumed its eventual shape because of liturgical needs. Taking the Prophet Muhammad's house in Medina as its starting-point, the Arab-style mosque had a wide but shallow sanctuary which fronted an open courtyard with a covered cloister on the other three sides. Known as the hypostyle mosque, this simple form also had certain requirements, foremost amongst which was the need for a directional pointer towards Mecca. This was followed by the need for some elevation to enable the leader of the Friday prayer to be both seen and heard; running water for the requisite ablutions before prayer; a high place from which the call to prayer could be given; and in certain major mosques, an area in which the ruler could pray in safety. These various requirements were realised by the *mihrab*, the *minbar*, the ablutions fountain, the minaret and the *maqsura*. The mihrab, originally a simple niche which indicated the direction of prayer, soon became the focus of decorative attention within the mosque, whilst as its height increased, the minaret began to attract functions other than that of simply the place for broadcasting the call to prayer and became both a lighthouse and a look-out tower.

The various liturgical requirements having been satisfied, the size and exact configuration of the mosque were apparently of little import. Flexibility was achieved by an additive use of the space unit which, in the case of the Arab hypostyle sanctuary, was the area between four columns, or, in the case of Iran, piers. By adding more sets of these space-creating elements – the roof-supporting columns or piers – greater space was easily created to meet the demands of an expanding congregation; the resultant unbalanced building was apparently quite acceptable. Facades which would define, and thereby confine, the mosque did not appear until the tenth century. Interesting examples of this type of addition to the Arab style mosque occur both at Nayin and, as demonstrated by recent archaeological work, at Siraf.

This Arab-style mosque, with its low but wide profile, was the one adopted in Iran, the only major difference being the replacement of the roof columns by piers, solid masonry supports. Columns were an obvious choice for any building in Mediterranean lands, which were littered with antique columns from earlier times, but these were unavailable in Iran, where brick or stone piers were introduced to replace the single supporting column. Comparatively rare examples of stone piers are seen in the 'Abbasid mosques at Shushtar and Siraf, while early examples of brick piers are extant in the Tarik Khana at Damghan and in the mosque at Nayin.

For the hundred years from the time of the conquest until the fall of the Umayyad dynasty in 750, Iran was ruled by a series of governors sent from the Caliph's court in Syria. It was a time of oppression for non-Arabs and converts, particularly in the outlying parts of the empire, so much so that it was the non-Arab inhabitants of the eastern part of the Iranian lands who were instrumental in the fall of the Umayyads and the establishment of the new 'Abbasid Caliphate. The capital was now moved from Syria to Baghdad in Iraq where much greater direct control was exercised by the Caliph and despite initial turbulence and rebellions the early period was comparatively peaceful. During this period Persian influence and traditions at court steadily advanced. Local Persian governors attained considerable power and a number of them began a series of semi-independent dynasties owing merely nominal allegiance to the Caliph.

It was the ninth century that saw the emergence of several of these independent principalities. In general their surviving buildings are of little importance to the development of architecture but two exceptions are those of the Samanids and the Buyids. The Samanids ruled in the eastern Iranian world in what is now Soviet Central Asia from about 875 until the end of the tenth century, and were of Persian descent. At their court a Persian renaissance began to take place, particularly associated with the use of Modern Persian as a literary medium. Bukhara and Samarqand became great centres of learning and art, and the tomb of the Samanid Isma'il in Bukhara remains a crucial monument in the study of the whole of eastern Islamic architecture. For Iran's history, the Samanids saw the important development of the Central Asian Turks as a cohesive force.

The Buyids were another Persian family, originally from the mountainous area south of the Caspian. Claiming descent from the ancient kings of Persia, they were also Shi'ite, that is followers of that minority form of Islam which takes its authority through the heirs of the family of Muhammad and which is that largely followed in Iran today. Emerging from their mountain fastnesses about the year 932, they eventually overran central and southern Iran as well as Iraq where, despite their outward homage, the Caliph himself was their client. Under the Buyids the Persian element which had already appeared with the Samanids also assumed important proportions. 'Adud ad-Dawla (949–982), perhaps the greatest of the Buyids, deliberately set out to assume all the appurtenances of one of the ancient kings, which included patronage of architecture; literary accounts of his reign abound with references to his building activities. Comparatively few Buyid monuments remain but those which do indicate a high artistic awareness and a groping towards the creation of a new building style making use of a number of techniques which were to be absorbed by successive waves of rulers from Central Asia.

Contemporary with the later Buyids, north-eastern Iran saw the appearance of the first Central Asian Turkish dynasty of the eastern Islamic world, the Ghaznavids (977–1186). Originally Turkish slaves of the Samanids, the Ghaznavids established themselves as independent rulers of Afghanistan and eastern Iran. Unlike the Buyids, they were Sunnis, that is belonging to the main group of Islam, and indeed carved out their Iranian provinces at the expense of the Buyids whom they attacked as secular and religious rivals. Their Iranian provinces were finally lost to the Saljuqs in 1040, whereupon they turned further east to establish an empire in northern India which lasted almost two hundred years.

The advent of the Saljuqs, who defeated both the Buyids and the Ghaznavids to rule all Iran, constitutes an historical date of absolute time, but paradoxically the architectural developments associated with them constitute relative time since they pre-date that arrival. An analysis of the monuments should help to make this distinction clearer.

Of the monuments still remaining from the period up to the arrival of the Saljuqs, mosques and tombs predominate. Literary sources provide descriptions of other buildings and archaeological investigations have produced additional information. From these various sources it is possible to reconstruct the course of architectural development during this period.

The oldest extant mosque in Iran is the Tarik Khana at Damghan. Although much restored, it is generally accepted to date, in its original form, from the eighth century. It has an almost square courtyard surrounded by a single tunnel-vaulted arcade with a deeper sanctuary. It is majestically simple in effect, but the brick piers and slightly pointed arches look back to an earlier pre-Islamic Sasanian original. However, the plan of the mosque is in the Arab style already described.

The old city of Nishapur which was so completely destroyed by the Mongols, apparently possessed a mosque which adhered to the Arab plan. The great mosque at Shushtar, originally founded in 866 under the 'Abbasids, is stone-built, again in the Arab style. Both this mosque and that at Siraf, also in stone, stand out of the mainstream of architectural development in Iran. They look more towards western Islamic forms. Although Shushtar has a later fifteenth-century minaret of great interest, for more intrinsically Iranian developments one must turn to the city of Isfahan.

Little remains in Isfahan from this early period, but that which does is of great importance. The Jurjir portal is the sole remnant of a great Buyid mosque to which it was attached, and it shows two important aspects of brick decoration already present in the tenth century. The whole of the portal is covered with stucco, but shows two different tendencies. In one series of patterns this follows the shape of the bricks themselves, making no attempt to disguise their form; the patterns are therefore created by the play of the bricks. This is the technique which is also essentially followed by the recently discovered columns of the old Buyid Jami' mosque in Isfahan. The other pattern form in the Jurjir portal emphasises surface over shape by means of the same medium, stucco. The designs built up by brick and stucco bear no relationship to the actual brick construction of the pilasters and other areas they cover.

The most striking example of this latter technique is in the Jami' mosque at Nayin where the sanctuary pillars are covered with carved and richly ornamented stucco which is totally divorced from the shape underneath. This use of stucco as a surface modifier, being as free as possible from the monument's physical properties, goes back to the Sasanian use of stucco, and was one of the essential ingredients of early Islamic decoration. At Nayin too, however, some of the brick columns around the courtyard are ornamented with patterns formed from the bricks themselves as in the Jami' mosque in Isfahan.

Therefore already within the Isfahan area in the tenth century there are two tendencies in pattern, one looking back to the earlier trends which link Iran with Iraq and Afghanistan, all following the Sasanian imperial style, the other revealing a new form of realism which abandons the essentially Persian concern for surface to stress that the surface relates directly to the construction itself. It is this latter form which appears to relate directly to the ideas and forms developing in Central Asia and which was to triumph in the eleventh and twelfth centuries under the Saljuqs.

One other interesting mosque form must be mentioned at this time: the *ivan* type. At Nayriz the original mosque dates back to the tenth century but has suffered many restorations, despite this, however, its basic plan still remains. This comprises a single great ivan, a barrel-vaulted three-sided rectangular chamber opening onto a courtyard. This ivan form has an ancient Persian origin and its appearance at this stage may be linked to the national revival already mentioned. In fact, a new type of mosque plan was created under the Saljuqs utilising a combination of the Arab plan, the old Persian ivan and a form of kiosk mosque which appeared in the eleventh century.

Early Islam did not encourage the construction of tombs, insisting on equality in death. This was at variance with pre-Islamic traditions, and by the tenth century these traditions were reasserting themselves. The Buyids constructed magnificent tomb towers, as at Ray where unfortunately they remain only as archaeological sites. However, the beginning of the eleventh century saw the creation of one of the most incredible tombs, not only in Iran but anywhere, the monumentally simple Gunbad-i Qabus. This building in northeastern Iran was built by one of the Ghaznavid vassal princes. The sheer monumentality of this tomb, with its complete honesty of construction and stark simplicity, contrasts with a contemporary group of tombs in the Mazandaran mountains. These look back to Sasanian times, even with inscriptions in Pahlavi (Middle Persian), indicating the tenacious hold of pre-Islamic Iranian traditions in the area.

In Damghan there are two notable monuments from the pre-Saljuq eleventh century, the Pir-i 'Alamdar tomb tower and the minaret of the Tarik Khana. Both use brick patterns which emphasise form over surface, that is they are directly related to the essential brick structure. Again they may be connected to the advent of Turkish power in that they were erected within the Ghaznavid sphere of power. They contain most of the brick patterns which were subsequently used to such remarkable effect by the Saljuqs, not only in other monuments in Damghan but throughout the Saljuq empire.

The Davazdah Imam tomb of the early eleventh century in Yazd has always been regarded as particularly important because in it is found the first appearance in Iran of the tri-lobed squinch, a device which tackles the problem of placing a dome on a square chamber. It has been suggested that if the Ribat-i Mahi caravanserai in the northeast in fact pre-dates the Yazd monument, a fact under scholarly discussion, some of the unusual squinches there might be forerunners of the tri-lobed squinch. This matter is now largely academic since the recent discovery in Soviet Central Asia of fully-developed tri-lobed squinches in a tenth-century mausoleum, the Arab Ata. Thus the Davazdah Imam may have been influenced by pre-Saljuq Central Asian ideas.

The minaret form which appeared in the eleventh century and which can be categorised as the eastern minaret form is also likely to have a Central Asian origin. It has been suggested that earlier minarets were either constructed of wood or of sun-dried mud-brick, which would help to account for their disappearance. The oldest remaining minaret in Iran is that of the Jami' mosque at Nayin. Here the solid square base and tapering octagonal shaft look back to the western minaret form, a supposition which its almost total lack of decoration tends to corroborate. The next minaret in chronological sequence reveals a considerable change and would indicate a shift of influence. The minaret and tomb at Sangbast can be dated to the early part of the eleventh century, certainly before 1028, the date of the death of Arslan Jadhib, the Ghaznavid official who apparently constructed them. The decorative scheme of the conico-cylindric minaret has both an inscription, unfortunately now illegible, and a number of simple patterns which were to become standard under the Saljuqs.

Thus even prior to the appearance of the Saljuqs in Iran the basic forms and patterns which they turned to such creative purposes had already appeared. The Saljuqs' genius lay in their understanding of these forms and the way in which they continued and enhanced their development.

From the Saljuqs to the coming of the Mongols (1040–c. 1220)

The Saljuqs were Turkish nomads originating in Central Asia who migrated to the area around Bukhara during the early eleventh century. About this time they embraced Sunni Islam. They participated in various dynastic wars and eventually felt themselves strong enough to challenge the Ghaznavids whom they defeated in 1040. They continued to overthrow most of the dynasties in Iran, Iraq, and Syria, and initiated the turkification of Anatolia. Thus, for the first time since the great days of the Caliphs, the whole eastern Islamic world was controlled by one dynasty.

Coming from a nomadic background with little idea of the complex bureaucracy needed to run an empire, the Saljuqs were dependent on the already existing apparatus, so that the empire was administered by Persians. As Sunnis, the Saljuqs were anxious to defend their orthodoxy, and in their fight against the propaganda of heterodox Shi'ism they developed the *madrasa*, a form of theological college, to train Sunni leaders. Few traces of the structures of these early madrasas survive in Iran although texts speak of many being founded there. The earliest remains are stucco fragments from the so-called Nizamiyya at Khargird. The so-called Haydariyya Madrasa in Qazvin has a late twelfth-century dome-chamber, but whether or not this originally functioned as a madrasa is unclear.

The empire of the Great Saljuqs lasted in Iran until the mid-twelfth century although Saljuq rulers continued in Iraq and southern Iran until almost the end of the century. Thereafter Iran was absorbed into the empire of the Khwarazmshahs, another Turkish dynasty emanating from the Oxus delta. They created a large empire in a short space of time but were destroyed by the Mongols from about 1220 on.

Custom refers to the whole of this period as Saljuq but neither actual nor relative time is in accord with this. Actual time must take account of the Khwarazmshah empire, and relative time the appearance of artistic and architectural forms and ideas which originated in the second half of the twelfth century and continue into the Mongol period.

Architecturally the period is characterised by the finest use of brick and brick decoration combined with a richly inventive carved stucco and terracotta. The stucco designs were organised along architectural lines, with finely carved mihrabs filling panels in mosques, and were usually painted in blue, red, white and green. This use of colour allied itself with tilework and terracotta to produce the first architectural use of coloured tiles within this period.

A series of examples of the great Iranian mosque form remains which utilises four ivans around the courtyard combined with monumental dome chambers. These latter first appeared as independent structures known as kiosk mosques but were soon absorbed into the main mosque form. The question of the origin of the four ivan mosque form has been much discussed but certainly the ivan itself is an Iranian invention which appears to have been transplanted to Central Asia during the Sasanian period. Apparently the four ivan form was used in a number of Buddhist monasteries in Central Asia and was again re-introduced when Turkish dynasties came to power.

Another Iranian invention which flourished during this period was the squinch. Used to transform a square chamber into an octagon on which a dome could be placed, this resolution of the problem was achieved during the first two centuries A.D. in Iran. It was used both in Iran and Central Asia prior to the Saljuqs, but it was they who turned it from an architectural solution into a significant artistic form.

There was also an upsurge in mysticism, Sufism, which affected architecture. The desire for private prayer led to the creation of many smaller mosques, which, of course, also gave an opportunity for the display of private piety, and also resulted in a proliferation of mihrabs within a single mosque. Perhaps the foremost example of this is the Paminar mosque in Zavara, which has seven mihrabs, but most major mosques had at least two side mihrabs in addition to the main one in the great dome chamber. A further consequence of Sufi movements was an increase in tombs and shrines which became objects of pilgrimage and veneration.

As has been shown, the earlier Islamic disapproval of tombs was submerged and they became an increasingly important architectural form. Initially they were erected mainly by rulers and local governors. Soon important tombs were built for various holy men and mystics which quickly became shrines. To these must be added monuments erected over the descendants of the Prophet, the Imams. Thus arose a body of monuments known as *imamzadas*, literally 'sons of Imams', a name by which the vast majority of saintly tombs are still known in Iran. Whilst this architectural form did not originate under the Saljuqs, it gathered momentum during this period, although it did not reach its full development until later.

Tomb towers and shrines appeared in a number of places in Saljuq Iran but it was the ubiquitous minaret which was brought to perfection at this time. Forty minarets still remain from pre-Mongol Iran; for their imaginative use of brickwork in all its manifold possibilities they are unsurpassed. The western minaret form, which had its origins in the square Syrian church towers, utilises the interior space, even providing windows in order that such space could be fully employed. The eastern minaret, as developed in pre-Mongol Iran, acknowledges interior space merely as a means of ascent, so that these tall slender towers, reaching for the sky, are more religious or commemorative affirmations than practical constructions.

Both form and overall decoration owe their origins to Central Asia, but the actual building methods were those of Iranian craftsmen who had learned their techniques in previous centuries. The final perfection of brickwork technique was a combination of inspiration and craftsmanship. High octagonal or square bases were surmounted by cylindrical or conico-cylindric shafts which were ornamented with a series of imaginative geometric patterns executed in brick, terracotta and stucco. Inscriptions in majestic scripts exhorted the faithful to prayer or lauded the munificence or piety of the donor. The patterns themselves utilised the strong sunlight of the region to make play with shadows so that the slow movement of the sun caused a corresponding three-dimensional rippling play of light on the surface of the minarets.

This mastery of brick technique was applied to all the great monuments including the magnificent series of caravanserais which linked the cities of the empire for both trade and pilgrimage, purposes which were again associated with the minaret. In these regions where much summer travel is done at night to avoid the heat of the day, directional indicators are essential, and these were provided by a light burning at the top of the minaret making them literally places of light or lighthouses. Indeed some were built as towers outside towns and served just this purpose, whereas the majority were attached to mosques and also used for the call to prayer.

The Saljuq contribution, therefore, consisted less in innovation than in imaginative utilisation of already existing techniques, combining Central Asian inspiration with the old craftsmanship of the Persians. This applied equally to techniques of government as well as to architecture. It was the Saljuqs who brought both to full fruition, and it was this spirit which permeated the age and continued after it. However, by the second half of the twelfth century the initial inspiration was fading, and a new artistic injection was provided by the Khwarazmshahs.

Colour made its first appearance architecturally with the Saljuqs, but the Khwarazmshahs used it to greater effect, although few buildings remain from the period to demonstrate this; brickwork also acquired a more massive quality, and both this and colour were traits continued under the Mongols. Again northeastern Iran's importance needs to be stressed. This area, Khurasan, was the richest area both intellectually and artistically and by its direct contact with Central Asia was the region where many of the new ideas first appeared. And it was in this area that the Mongols struck hardest.

The Mongols (c. 1220–1353)

The first appearance of the Mongols in Iran was totally destructive. Within a short time the Khwarazmshah empire was destroyed, its ruler dead and his son a fugitive until his murder in 1231. Major territorial acquisition was not a feature of Mongol policy in Iran until Hulagu, grandson of Chingiz Khan, advanced to destroy the hitherto impregnable castles of the Shi'a sect of the Assassins whose main centres lay in the mountains south of the Caspian. He continued on to Baghdad, which he destroyed in 1258 and slew the last legitimate 'Abbasid Caliph so ending their dynasty. The Mongol advance was finally halted in Syria by Mamluk troops from Egypt. Hulagu remained in Iran to consolidate his possessions and founded a dynasty known as the Il Khanid.

At this stage the Mongols were not Muslims but were very tolerant in religious matters. Many were Christian or Buddhist and initially the few that inclined towards Islam often had wives of other religions. During their early years there was little architectural activity, for the Mongols continued living in tented encampments, moving with the seasons. However, by the end of the century coinciding with their conversion to Islam, these encampments were exchanged for less ephemeral cities. As under the Saljuqs their bureaucracy was in Persian hands, and much of the building activity was inspired by rivalry between different ministers, whilst the rulers also built in the Persian tradition.

The Mongol period was characterised by open communication between Iran, Central Asia and China. At this time Iran was part of an empire stretching from the confines of Europe across Asia to China, with a corresponding increase in trade and the opportunity to travel. This was reflected in the arts, but more particularly in design patterns than in major architectural forms. Direct allegiance to the senior Mongol ruler in China was ended by 1300, but this had little effect on the continued cultural interchange.

The early fourteenth century saw the high point of Mongol rule in Iran. Intellectual progress, especially in the sciences, was made and architecture was greatly patronised. Possibly as a result of the devastation caused by the first Mongol invasions, this period saw a shift of emphasis from northeast to northwest Iran where Tabriz became a main centre. Two new cities were constructed in this region of which little remains, but in addition to the great tomb of Sultaniyya – one of Iran's great monuments – there are for the first time detailed accounts by European travellers of these cities both in prosperity and decay.

Apart from remains of a religious nature, there are the meagre remnants of at least one palace and accounts of the new quarters in the various cities. These remains point to a remarkable continuity despite the break caused by the invasions. Architecture apparently progressed from the point at which it had somewhat abruptly ceased, continuing the technique and developing the forms and ideas of the preceding age.

Briefly, under the Saljuqs architectural emphasis had lain on structure; even decoration was based on form and integrated with the innate structure of the building. This emphasis runs counter to the Iranian ethos which has always maintained an interest in ornamental surface that is at least equal to structural form, while the latter probably drew on the influence of the Central Asian Turks. Under the Mongols, intrinsic Iranian attitudes again came to the fore with greater emphasis on surface, although such decoration was

still more closely related to structure than in subsequent centuries. Designs and patterns continued a long-established tradition only developing by the more intense and imaginative use of colour in various techniques. Even this, however, was still balanced, maintaining a harmony between surface and form, or rather between the architectural surface and the surface decoration.

The lack of concern with basic structural form showed in the materials used. Walls were constructed of rubble and then covered with a film of stucco which was then incised to represent actual brick patterns, a technique which would have been rejected in the previous age. This idea reflected a movement away from the massive construction of the Saljuq period to a lighter, more vertical constructional form. The great dome chambers became higher and lighter in feeling with the strength concentrated only at precisely important load-bearing points; intervening walls were not only more flimsy but were pierced with wider and loftier openings.

Decoration itself was the main beneficiary of Mongol architectural development. This was applied to buildings after construction, apparently using detailed plans. Stucco acquired an even richer vocabulary and was in turn painted with brilliant colours. However, the great advance was in the production of coloured tiles, which were applied to the interiors of mosques, tombs and palaces. In addition to the use of superb turquoise and dark lapis lazuli blues, even ornamented with real gold, the technique of lustre painting was perfected. A series of great lustre-painted mihrabs was produced with surrounding dados of lustre tiles, the whole combined with painted stucco to produce an effect of incomparable richness.

Thus during the whole period covered, an

unbroken continuity of architectural achievement is seen. Forms and ideas native to Iran were established prior to the Turks' arrival. A body of tradition and craftsmanship was available which was able to realise the ideas and inspiration from Central Asia. These found form and solidarity under the Saljuqs, so that by the beginning of the thirteenth century the basic form of the Iranian mosque had been worked out and structuralised. By the end of the Mongol period the basic form had almost achieved its final proportions and a start had been made in the use of colour which was eventually to become the perfect medium for Persian expression. While in principle this line of development can be said to be unbroken, the final achievements often occur at the fall of a dynasty so that the crescendo is somehow missed. This had to wait until the Persian feeling for colour and decoration finally fused with the form and structure which had been elaborated over previous centuries.

Time Chart

Important Historical Events	Notable Buildings
632 Death of Muhammad.	
750 Victory of the 'Abbasids.	8th century, Damghan, Tarik Khana founded.
	866 Shushtar, Jami' Mosque.
945 Buyids enter Baghdad.	Isfahan, Jurjir Portal and Tomb Towers at Ray and Samiran.
998–1030 Zenith of Ghaznavids.	1006 Gunbad-i Qabus.
	1027 Tarik Khana minaret.
	1028 Sangbast, Arslan Jadhib tomb and minaret.
1055 Saljuqs enter Baghdad.	
	1061–2 Sava, Maydan Minaret.
1072 Accession of Saljuq Sultan Malikshah.	Period of great dome chambers as at Isfahan, Gulpaygan and Ardistan.
	1110–11 Sava, Jami' Mosque Minaret.
	1121 Isfahan Jami' Mosque acquires four ivans.
	1135 four-ivan mosque at Zawara.
	1154 Ribat-i Sharaf restored.
1157 Death of Sanjar, the last great Saljuq ruler.	
1194 Last Saljuq in Iran defeated by Khwarazmshahs.	1219 Zuzan Mosque.
1220 Mongol invasions begin.	
1256 Hulagu founds Il Khans.	Early 14th century: shrines at Linjan, Bistam and Natanz.
1317 Death of Uljaytu.	Sultaniyya, Tomb of Uljaytu.
	1322 Varamin, Jami' Mosque.
1336 on sees the effective end of the Il Khans.	

Selected Glossary

'Abbasids	749–1258, Sunni dynasty of Caliphs, ruling from Baghdad.
Buyids	932–1062, Persian Shi'ite dynasty from northern Iran whose members ruled most of Persia and Iraq until the advent of the Saljuqs.
Ghaznavids	977–1186, dynasty ruling Khurasan, Afghanistan and later northern India, and the first of Central Asian Turkish origin in eastern Islam.
Hajj	The annual pilgrimage to Mecca.
Il Khans	1256–1353, the Mongol rulers of Iran.
Imamzada	Literally 'son of the Imams', signifying a holy or saintly person and more particularly his tomb.
Ivan	Rectangular chamber open on one side usually surmounted by a barrel vault.
Jami'	Usually translated as 'congregational', a term applied to an important mosque where the Friday noon prayer was led from the pulpit (minbar).
Khwarazmshahs	About 1077–1231, Central Asian rulers around the Oxus Delta whose power extended into Iran towards the end of the twelfth century before their defeat by the Mongols.
Madrasa	School, and more particularly a type of theological college.
Maqsura	An area in a mosque so designed that the ruler could pray in safety and free from fear of assassination attempts.
Mihrab	Niche, usually in a religious building, indicating the direction of Mecca and hence of prayer.
Minbar	The equivalent of a pulpit located in Jami' mosques; the Friday noon prayer is led from the minbar.
Mongols	Central Asian invaders who conquered much of the civilised world including most of eastern Islam from 1220.
Saljuqs	1038–1194, Central Asian Turks who ruled Iran, Iraq and adjacent areas.
Samanids	819–1005, Persian dynasty ruling Transoxiana and eastern Iran.
Sasanians	The pre-Islamic rulers of Iran and Iraq before their conquest by the Arabs in the middle of the seventh century.
Shi'a (adj. Shi'ite)	The branch of Islam which supports the spiritual authority descended through the family of the Prophet, and opponents of the Sunnis.
Sunna (adj. Sunni)	The branch of Islam which supports the authority of the most able person within the Prophet's tribe.
Umayyads	661–750, Caliphal dynasty controlling most of Islam from Syria.

Short Bibliography

Cambridge History of Iran vols. IV and V, CUP, 1975 and 1968
Diez E. *Churasanische Baudenkmäler* Berlin, 1918
Godard A. *The Art of Iran* London, 1965
Hill D. and O. Grabar *Islamic Architecture and its Decoration, AD 800–1500* (2nd edition), London, 1967
Leacroft H. and R. *The Buildings of Early Islam* London, 1976
Lewis B. *The World of Islam* London, 1976
Matheson S. A. *Persia: An Archaeological Guide* London, 1972
Pope A. U. *Persian Architecture* London, 1965
Pope A. U. *A Survey of Persian Art* 6 vols., London and New York, 1938–9
Scerrato U. *Monuments of Civilization: Islam* London, 1976
Wilber D. N. *The Architecture of Islamic Iran. The Il-Khanid Period* Princeton, 1955

The following periodicals also contain articles relevant to this period of Islamic architecture in Iran:

AARP Art and Archaeology Research Papers, London
Ars Islamica Ann Arbor, Mich.
Ars Orientalis Ann Arbor, Mich.
Athar-i Iran Tehran
Der Islam Berlin
East and West Rome
Iran, the Journal of the British Institute of Persian Studies London and Tehran
The Journal of the Royal Asiatic Society London

Index

Plate 1 Gunbad-i Qabus, Tomb Tower. This great 55 metre high brick tower was
built as a tomb by Qabus ibn Vashmgir from 1006–7. Excavations into the massive
foundations found no trace of a tomb, lending credence to the legend that Qabus' body
was suspended from the roof in a glass coffin.

33

Plate 2 Shushtar, the Jami'
Mosque. Originally begun in 866 by
an 'Abbasid Caliph this mosque is
remarkable for its stone construction,
with great stone piers supporting the
roof in the sanctuary.

Plate 3 Nayin, the Jami' Mosque. Built around the middle of the tenth century, this is one of the oldest Iranian mosques still in regular use. The facade of the courtyard is ornamented with simple brick patterns.

Plate 4 Damghan, the Minaret of the Jami' Mosque. Probably the first minaret actually built under the Saljuqs around 1058, it has some of the finest raised brick patterns, the strong sunlight creating an intricate shadow-play.

Plate 5 Kirat, Minaret. This isolated minaret was undoubtedly used as a watchtower and a lighthouse. The remains of a balcony above the high octagonal base would also indicate that it was used for the call to prayer, implying the existence of a nearby mosque and village. The varied and beautiful brick patterns would suggest a date around 1100.

Plate 6 Gulpaygan, the Jami'
Mosque. The dome chamber of this
mosque is dated 1104–1118 and was
originally a separate kiosk mosque,
the remainder of the mosque being a
nineteenth century addition. The
squinch exterior is clearly shown at
the transition from the square
chamber to the octagonal dome
support.

Plate 7 Sava, the Minaret of the Jami' Mosque. Probably the finest of all Iranian Saljuq minarets this is dated 1110. It has a series of exquisite raised brick pattern bands alternating with brick inscriptions which cover the entire shaft except for the modern restoration.

Plate 8 Ardistan, the Jami' Mosque. This mosque has at least four building periods. Started before the Saljuqs, the dome chamber was then built between 1072–92, and converted into a four-ivan mosque in 1160, while the madrasa was added much later.

Plate 10 Ribat-i Sharaf. This magnificent royal caravanserai on the road between Khurasan and Samarqand was first built about 1120 and then restored in 1154. The high portal complex is decorated with superb brick patterns and has a small mihrab to one side so that travellers who arrived after the gates were closed would know the direction of prayer.

Plate 11 Kirman, Jabal-i Sang. Meaning 'Mountain of Stone', this domed chamber is one of the most majestic monuments of southern Iran and one of the most puzzling. Neither its date nor use can be determined with certainty, but it probably dates from the late twelfth century and was possibly never finished.

Plate 12 Maragha, Gunbad-i Kabud, Tomb Tower. This tower was always ascribed to the mother of the first Il Khanid ruler, Hulagu, but the portal inscription gives a date of 1196, 60 years before the coming of the Il Khans. The damaged inscription in turquoise blue tilework is set between brick guard bands, while more tile mosaic is used to highlight the ornamental brick patterns which cover the entire surface of the tower.

Plate 13 Nigar, the Jami' Mosque. This small village has a mosque with a minaret from the beginning of the thirteenth century boasting one of the earliest and most beautiful inscriptions in turquoise tile mosaic.

Plate 14 Radkan, Tomb Tower. Built between 1280 and 1300 in northern Khurasan, this is the first tomb tower in Iran to have a series of engaged half-columns on the exterior. An inscription in light blue glazed terracotta encircles the tower below the conical roof, but has been damaged in a number of places.

Plate 15 Damavand, the Imamzada 'Abd Allah. Unfortunately the entire upper section of this tomb tower has been restored, all the blue glazed bricks being modern, but the general style would suggest a date around 1300. The actual form is unusual in that the exterior is surrounded with 33 pointed flanges, all of which, including the interior dome, are original.

Plate 16 Sarvistan, the Imamzada of Shaykh Yusuf. This elegant tomb has some very fine stone carving and is supported on monolithic stone pillars. The finely carved sarcophagus of the Shaykh is dated 1283, and the monument bears dates from 1281 to 1349.

Plate 17 'Aliabad Kishmar, Tomb Tower. The exterior of this tomb tower is adorned with a series of flanges alternating with half-round columns. These were originally highlighted with glazed terracotta insets in light and dark blue, most of which have now disappeared. There is no dating inscription, but it would appear to have been built about 1300.

Plate 18 Isfahan, the Mihrab of Uljaytu in the Jami' Mosque. This superb mihrab of carved stucco is dated 1310 and is one of the finest remaining. Its elegant inscriptions are picked out in white and raised so as to stand out against the richly carved light ochre background.

Plate 19 Sultaniyya, Mausoleum of Uljaytu. Uljaytu reigned from 1304 until 1317 during which period he built this impressive tomb as the centrepiece of a new city. The exterior is ornamented with a series of decorative panels in light and dark blue glazed bricks, while the ceiling of the gallery which runs below the base of the dome has vaults covered with polychrome plaster. (Photo: Warwick Ball.)

Plate 20 Ashtarjan, the Jami'
Mosque. The high portal of this
mosque is surmounted by the
truncated stumps of two minarets
decorated with an inscription
formed of turquoise and cobalt blue
glazed bricks. The portal itself is
ornamented with tile mosaic patterns
and an inscription giving the date
1315.

Plate 21 Natanz, the Jami'
Mosque and Shrine Complex of
Shaykh 'Abd as-Samad. Constructed
around the tomb of the Shaykh, the
complex was begun in 1304 and the
minaret completed in 1324. There is a
rich use of tile mosaic throughout,
and the picture shows a stalactite-
headed niche flanked by
inscriptions in seal script with a
further cursive inscription in white
against a blue patterned
background.

Plate 22 Varamin, the Jami' Mosque. The silhouette of the great dome dominates this beautiful four-ivan mosque, the only one remaining from the Mongol period to have been designed and built as such in one construction period. Two inscriptions give the dates 1322 and 1326. (Photo: Warwick Ball.)

Plate 23 Isfahan, Bagh-i Qush Khana Minaret. This minaret probably originally formed one of a pair over a monumental portal, a common feature of the Mongol period. The other buildings of the original complex have now disappeared, but the glazed brick decoration on the base and the shaft would suggest a date between 1330 and 1350.

Plate 24 Sirjan, the Tomb of Shah Firuz. This domed brick octagonal kiosk tomb is built on the top of a sheer rocky outcrop and has no inscriptions. It probably dates from the second half of the fourteenth century just before the whole area was devastated by Timur. A non-extant parapet would have given greater elegance to the dome outline, whilst the bases of the piers were originally joined to provide a brick platform.

Plates 1 and 2 Damghan, Tarik Khana Mosque, 8th century. This is the oldest extant mosque in Iran and although in the simple Arab plan it retains many elements recalling Iran's pre-Islamic heritage. The massive piers and the shape of the arches follow Sasanian prototypes. Although its foundation dates from the eighth century and it has been restored on several occasions, the mosque still keeps its original plan and impressive simplicity.

Plate 3 Isfahan, Jurjir Portal, 10th century. The portal was originally part of a tenth century Buyid mosque but now adjoins the much later Hakim Mosque. Stucco covers the whole portal with a number of remarkable patterns. The top of the wall below the divided semi-dome has a simple monumental inscription.

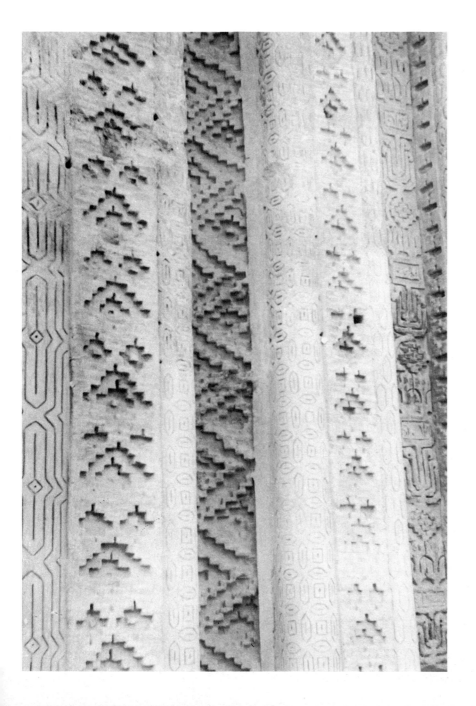

Plate 5 Isfahan, Jurjir Portal, detail, 10th century. The two decorative styles are shown in this section of the portal, demonstrating the existence of both tendencies at this period. It was the second which was to be brought to such heights in the succeeding Saljuq era when the Central Asian Turks utilised Iranian technical mastery to achieve a magnificent synthesis. (Photo: L. Harrow.)

Plate 6 Samiran, Tomb Tower, 10th century. Probably built by the Buyids, this stone-built tomb tower is one of a group situated in the Alburz mountains. The polygonal shape of the tower and its engaged columns foreshadow later developments in this type of building. Nearby are the remains of contemporary fortifications. (Photo: Warwick Ball.)

Plate 7 Nayin, Jami' Mosque Minaret, 10th century. This minaret is the oldest surviving in Iran. The tapering octagonal shaft in plain bond has practically no ornament.

Plates 8 and 9 Nayin, Jami' Mosque, arcade and mihrab detail, 10th century.
The piers of the mosque's arcades have brick-formed patterns integrating form and
decoration. The hood of the niche as with the whole mihrab and its adjacent arches
and piers is covered with exquisite stucco. The stucco's complex and detailed
patterns have their origins in early Islamic designs in Mesopotamia which in turn are
inspired by Sasanian stucco work.

Plate 10 Muhammadiyya, Sar-i Kucha Mosque, detail, 11th century. The mosque has an unusual plan descended from pre-Islamic barrel-vaulted structures and has numerous finely painted inscription friezes, whilst the dome above the rectangular sanctuary is carried on simple squinches.

Plate 11 Gunbad-i Qabus, Tomb Tower, 1006–7. This extraordinary structure which dominates the locality was conceived as a tomb but obviously served as a symbol of power for its builder Qabus. It is of fine brick with two bands of simple inscription. Only the base and parts of the roof have required any restoration.

Plate 12 Lajim, Tomb Tower, 1022. This circular brick tomb is one of a group of three situated in the Alburz Mountains in Mazandaran and was built by a semi-independent dynasty which traced its origins back to Sasanian Iran, a fact stressed by the bands of inscription: the lower band is in Arabic and the upper is in Pahlavi (Middle Persian).

Plate 13 Yazd, Davazdah Imam Mausoleum, 11th century. Now much restored the mausoleum bears the date 1036–7. Above the square chamber can be seen the shell-like exteriors of the squinches which create the octagon to support the dome. The tri-lobed squinches of this building are amongst the earliest of their type in Iran proper.

Plate 14 Sangbast, Arslan Jadhib Tomb, about 1028. Seen from the adjacent minaret, the tomb is probably that of a Ghaznavid official, Arslan, who died in 1028. The square chamber is surmounted by a dome through a deep zone of transition. About the tomb are the remains of former settlements.

Plate 15 Sangbast, Arslan Jadhib Tomb, interior, about 1028. Pierced by four pointed-arch windows the zone of transition uses a type of hooded squinch arch. Around the rim of the dome is a fine Arabic inscription. The dome itself is a notable example of brick technique with an interesting herringbone pattern.

Plate 16 Sangbast, Arslan Jadhib
Minaret, about 1028. The minaret is
22 metres high and in the eastern
tradition; it may once have been
part of a monumental portal.
Patterns are formed by the plain
bond of double stretchers. An
internal spiral staircase ascends to the
top where a balcony formerly
existed, supported by the two rows of
stalactites still visible.

Plate 17 Damghan, Pir-i 'Alamdar Tomb Tower, 1026–7. This important structure was built during a period when the area was controlled by vassals of the Ghaznavids. There are few traces of the mosque which stood by the tomb. The fine brick patterns on the tower were adopted in subsequent buildings both in Damghan and elsewhere.

Plate 18 Damghan Tarik Khana
Minaret, mid-11th century.
Probably dating from about 1027 and
thus prior to the Saljuqs, this
tapering cylindrical minaret is one of
the finest of its type. The shaft's six
zones of brick-formed patterns are
very complex and the effect of
sunlight with its deeply cast
shadows has a dramatic effect. The
minaret replaced an earlier square
structure probably contemporary
with the adjacent mosque.

Plate 19 Damghan, Chihil
Dukhtaran Tomb Tower, 1054–55.
Built during the ascendancy of the
Saljuqs, this tower with its complex
brick patterns continues the
tradition of such techniques
apparent in other contemporary
buildings in Damghan.

Plate 20 Nayriz, Jami' Mosque Minaret, 11th century. The foundation of the mosque was in 973–4, but this minaret may date from a rebuilding in 1067. It is about 30 metres high and the patterns formed by the bricks in the upper sections are very simple. The mosque itself is an interesting survival of an indigenous Iranian ivan-type.

Plate 21 Simnan, Jami' Mosque Minaret, 11th century. Probably built in the first half of the eleventh century, many of the beautiful brick patterns on the minaret are similar to those seen in the monuments at Damghan. The balcony rests on a projecting series of stalactites. Originally the minaret may have been freestanding.

Plate 22 Sava, Maydan Mosque Minaret, 1061–2. Now a truncated stump
adjoining a sixteenth century mosque, this is the earliest dated minaret in Iran.
The section above the inscription band is a late addition. The eight-pointed star
brick pattern is similar to that above the portal of the Shaykh Shibli tomb at
Damavand.

Plate 23 Damavand, Shaykh Shibli Tomb Tower, 11th century. Usually dated to the late eleventh century, the brick-built tomb is nearly 10 metres high. It is octagonal with rounded buttresses at the corners. Two pairs of niches surmount the door above which is a rectangular panel with eight-pointed star designs in brick.

Plate 24 Zavara, Paminar Mosque Minaret, 1068–9. Now about 21 metres high, the minaret was originally free-standing but was incorporated into the mosque during a later rebuilding. The inscription band is near the level of the present roof.

Plate 25 Zavara, Paminar Mosque Minaret, detail, 1068–9. The simple arrangement of bricks creates the decoration of the shaft. The remains of the cornice with its series of niches once supported a balcony where the call to prayer might be given.

Plate 26 Zavara, Paminar Mosque, detail, 11th and 13th/14th centuries. The sanctuary of the mosque has a number of mihrabs and adjacent areas decorated with some unusual stucco motifs. The various spiral patterns probably date from the Mongol period overlaying earlier Saljuq brickwork, a fragment of which can be seen in the corner of the squinch.

Plate 27 Mil-i Nadiri, Tower,
11th century. This tower seems to
have been built originally about 1070
by a local Saljuq ruler. Located in
the southeastern desert it served as a
landmark to guide travellers by night
or day. A restoration under Nadir
Shah (1736–47) gives it its present
name. It now stands 19.8 metres
high.

Plate 28 Kharraqan Tomb Tower, detail, 1067–8. One of a pair of anonymous Saljuq tombs, this detail is from the earlier one. It has an inscription frieze above which is an interesting geometric design. (Photo: Warwick Ball.)

Plate 29 Kirman, Malik Mosque
Minaret, 11th century.
Contemporary with the adjacent
mosque dating from the late
eleventh century, only about
7.5 metres remains. The inner core of
bricks beneath the outer layer
which forms the designs is here
visible.

Plates 30 and 31 Kashan, Jami'
Mosque Minaret and detail, 1073–4.
The mosque itself is an ancient
foundation but most of it now dates
from a later restoration. The
tapering minaret with an
inscription giving the date now
stands over 23 metres high although
the upper 5 metres is a later
addition. The minaret was originally
free-standing before being
enclosed within the later mosque.

Plate 32 Isfahan, Jami' Mosque, Great Dome Chamber, detail, about 1080.
Built during the reign of the Saljuq Malikshah, 1072–92, the chamber contains the
mihrab and was originally a free-standing building within the old mosque. Until
recently it was coated with plaster from a later period; restoration work has now
revealed the magnificence of the original Saljuq brickwork.

Plate 33 Isfahan, Jami' Mosque, arcade, 12th century. Located near the main entrance, the old arcades probably date from the Saljuq rebuilding after a fire in 1121. The domes supported by the columns have a rich variety of patterns created by the brickwork.

Plate 34 Isfahan, Jami' Mosque, ivan rear, about 1131. The ivans were part of the Saljuq rebuilding. Seen from the rear the apparently haphazard structure is the result of much rebuilding but the basic form of the original ivan structure is visible, untrammelled by any later decorative overlay.

Plate 35 'Ala Minaret, 11th century. This minaret is 10.25 metres high and probably dates from the late eleventh century. The shaft's brick decoration is very simple. Atop the minaret was originally a balcony. In design the minaret is not unlike that at Nayriz.

Plate 36 Kirat Minaret, late 11th century. In its elevated position it probably served as a signal tower as well as a place for the call to prayer as witnessed by the remains of a balcony above the octagonal base. It stands 24.6 metres high.

Plate 37 Kirat Minaret, detail, late 11th century. The octagonal base stands 16.45 metres high and has been subjected to some rough restoration. There are several bands of brick-formed patterns as well as an inscription although no date has been deciphered.

Plates 38 and 39 Barsiyan Mosque Minaret and detail, 1097. The minaret of 1097 was later surrounded by the mosque which dates from 1134. The minaret is 34.55 metres high and the shaft's decoration is comparatively simple with the bricks forming a diaper pattern. The depressed Greek crosses once contained stucco or terracotta insets and all the minaret's decoration was formerly picked out by stucco.

Plate 40 Takistan, Pir Mausoleum, about 1100. Now in the process of restoration this mausoleum has an interesting facade with blind arches flanking the door and both the niches and the entrance are surmounted by simple stalactite vaulting. (Photo: Warwick Ball.)

Plate 41 Isfahan, Chihil Dukhtaran Minaret, detail, 1107–8. The upper section of the shaft in plain bond with wide rising joints is pierced by an opening facing Mecca. The rectangular opening has a wooden lintel and is flanked by engaged colonnettes supporting a slightly concave tympanum. Through the opening can be seen the spiral staircase.

Plate 42 Sava, Jami' Mosque Minaret, 1110–11. This minaret whose lower section has been restored, is most richly decorated with complex raised brick patterns in numerous zones. Originally the minaret was also ornamented with a considerable amount of stucco.

Plate 43 Gulpaygan, Jami' Mosque, squinch, 1104–17. The square chamber supports the dome through the octagon formed by the squinches. Saljuq craftsmen transformed the simple squinch into a complicated poly-lobed form integrating brick and terracotta decoration into the structure.

Plate 44 Khusrawgird Minaret, 1111–12. Now having a total height of 28.5 metres, the minaret is dated by an inscription. The platform and base is a restoration and there is no indication of any former adjacent buildings. The shaft has numerous zones of pattern in the tradition of Saljuq brick decoration.

Plate 45 Bistam, Shrine of Bayazid Minaret, probably 1120–1. Situated within the shrine complex of the ninth century saint, Bayazid, the minaret is a fine example of Saljuq brick technique with deep zones of patterns. A cornice of three tiers at the top originally supported a balcony. The entire minaret is most richly decorated with stucco infills and brick plugs.

Plate 46 Qazvin, Jami' Mosque, 12th century. This four-ivan mosque contains much from later centuries but the great dome chamber was built about 1115, and is over 15 metres in diameter. The zone of transition is indicated by the exterior of the squinches. The exterior tiling is a later addition.

Plate 47 Qazvin, Jsmi' Mosque, interior detail, probably 12th century. The assumed lay of the brick construction forms patterns which are delicately carved in plaster. Some of the small brick plugs bear the name of God.

103

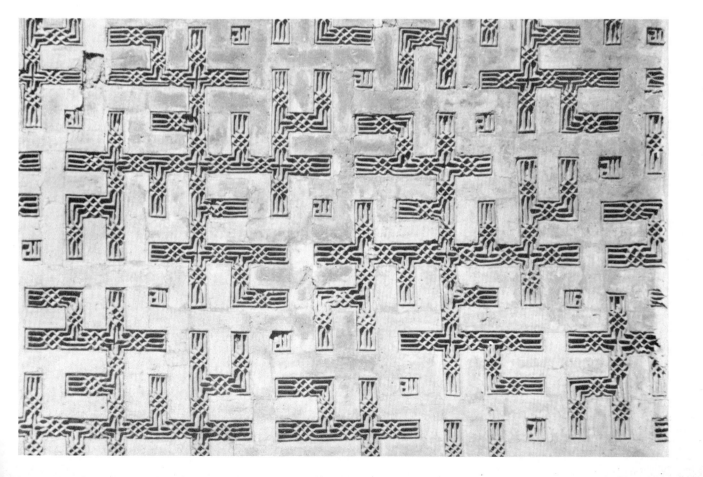

fine herringbone pattern and two inscription panels. The highly decorated
inscription is framed between guard bands of shaped brick. The guard bands and
inscriptions were formerly covered with stucco in order to clarify and emphasise
these zones.

Plates 50 and 51 Zavara, Jami'
Mosque, ivan and arcade, 1135. This
fine example of an early four–ivan
mosque is situated in an oasis town
on the edge of the central Iranian
desert. The plain brick arcades of its
courtyard are highlighted by a simple
monumental inscription while the
interior arcading of the dome
chamber is ornamented with
carved stucco panels and a superb
stucco mihrab.

Plate 52 Zavara, Jami' Mosque Minaret, 1135–6. Forming part of the original fabric of the mosque, the truncated shaft, 11.7 metres high, is set on an octagonal base. Included in the zones of brick-formed pattern is a restrained use of glazed bricks marking the appearance of colour as exterior ornament in such minarets.

Plate 53, Ardistan, Jami' Mosque, 11th century on. This important mosque was probably built on the site of a Sasanian fire temple. The great dome chamber dates from the reign of Malikshah, 1072–92. About 1160 four ivans were built around the courtyard to give it the classic form of the Iranian mosque.

Plates 54 and 55 Ardistan, Jami',
ivans, 12th century. The deep
barrel-vault of the ivan is faced on the
courtyard side by a monumental
facade which remains an important
element in Iranian Islamic
architecture. The vault and end wall
of the sanctuary ivan are overlayed
with a fine tracery of carved stucco.

Plate 56 Ardistan, Jami' Mosque Mihrab, 11th century. The use of stucco to decorate the dome chamber was brought to a peak under the Saljuqs as demonstrated by the superbly carved mihrab. The technique was to be continued under the Mongols but not surpassed.

Plate 57 Ardistan, Jami' Mosque, detail, 12th century. Adjacent to the dome chamber, the soffit of this arch is decorated with an inscription which is in an excellent state of preservation.

Plate 58 Ardistan, Jami' Mosque, squinch, between 1072 and 1092. The magnificent dome chamber shows Saljuq brickwork technique at its best. Unlike the poly-lobed squinch at Gulpaygan, those at Ardistan follow the more usual Saljuq form and are tri-lobed. A long inscription runs around the upper edge of the chamber.

Plate 59 Ardistan, Jami' Mosque Minaret, about 1160. Although the minaret is contemporary with the mosque's extension in 1160, it is likely that the upper section dates from a sixteenth century rebuilding. The present height is 13.31 metres.

Plate 60 Maragha, Gunbad-i
Surkh Tomb Tower, 1148.
Meaning 'the Red Tomb Tower' this
building rests on a stone base. The
panel above the door contains a fine
inscription with a restrained use of
colour.

Plate 61 Maragha, Gunbad-i Surkh Tomb, 1148. On the rear the brick bond forms the main decorative motifs in the blind arches and on the engaged columns. Running below the line of the roof is an elaborate inscription.

Plates 62 and 63 Khurasan, Ribat-i Mahi Caravanserai, 11th/12th century. As legend associates the structure with the Ghaznavid ruler Mahmud and the epic poet Firdawsi, it may date originally from the early eleventh century; but it was probably restored around 1154 when the nearby Ribat-i Sharaf was restored. Little remains of this caravanserai except the entrance portal, part of a dome chamber with unusual squinches, and traces of a fine inscription.

Plates 64 and 65 Ribat-i Sharaf Caravanserai, mid-12th century. At its construction about 1120 and restoration about 1154, no expense was spared to ensure the magnificence of this royal caravanserai. This is demonstrated by the rich brickwork decoration and inscription above the monumental entrance portal and the deeply carved stucco which embellishes the portal arch joining the two internal courtyards.

Plate 66 Ribat-i Sharaf Caravanserai, mid-12th century. The central ivan fronts a dome chamber which may have served as a royal reception hall, whilst the arched facades on either side conceal two self-contained palatial suites. The great arch is surmounted by a fine geometric pattern enclosed by a partially destroyed monumental inscription.

Plate 67 Gurgan, Jami' Mosque Minaret, 12th century. Although many of its decorative elements have been effaced during restoration this minaret is apparently Saljuq and its lower section is now encased in the later mosque building. The platform and tiled roof are of recent construction but typical of the style of this region lying to the south of the Caspian with its independent outlook.

Plate 68 Ardistan, Imam Hasan Mosque Minaret, 12th century. Now all that remains of a Saljuq madrasa, the minaret is probably late twelfth century. The present height of the minaret is about 13 metres although until recently there existed an upper section with brick patterns. The minaret was formerly one of a pair crowning a portal.

Plate 69 Tabas, Daw Minar Madrasa, late 12th century. The twin minarets crown the portal of a madrasa, rebuilt in the seventeenth century but probably following the original Saljuq plan of the twelfth century. The brick-formed patterns on the shaft were obliterated by restoration work some years ago. Around the shafts are bands of inscription picked out in blue glazed faience.

Plates 70 and 71 Kirman, Khwaja Atabeg Mausoleum, interior, 12th century. The mausoleum has an unusual plan being octagonal on the exterior and square inside. The interior is richly decorated with brick patterns and stucco overlay. There is some use of glazed faience insets and a series of monumental inscriptions.

Plate 72 Kuh-i Banan, Madrasa, 12th century. This partially ruined monument contains a number of pieces of fine stucco from the Saljuq period. Most of this is in a poor state but one of the mihrabs is almost complete. Recent restoration has preserved it.

Plate 73 Riza'iyya, Si Gunbad Tomb Tower, 1180. The tomb is circular with a rectangular doorway. The bricks form numerous patterns and a long inscription frames the entrance which is crowned by a semi-dome with a simple form of stalactite construction.

Plate 74 Isfahan, 'Ali Minaret, late 12th century. Nearly 48 metres high, this minaret is the tallest in Isfahan. The shaft bears patterns in brick and turquoise faience. An interesting feature is the use of cavetto cornices.

Plate 75 Isfahan, Rahravan Minaret, detail, 13th century. This minaret just pre-dates the Mongols. The shaft is simply decorated but has zones of decoration utilising glazed bricks of somewhat indifferent quality.

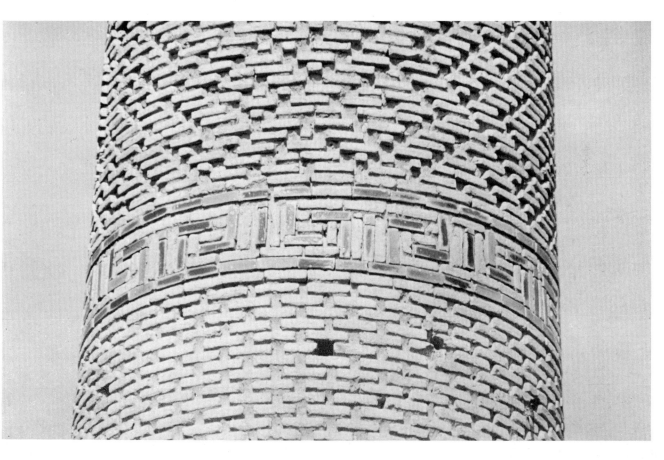

Plate 76 Gunabad, Jami' Mosque, 13th century. The mosque bears the date 1212 and was damaged by earthquake in 1968. In the Khurasan tradition there are only two ivans facing each other. The ivan's facade conceals the bases of two minarets which formerly crowned it.

Plate 77 Gunabad, Jami' Mosque, grille, probably 13th century. Located in the northeastern ivan, this interesting grille is made of shaped terracotta to form geometric patterns.

Plate 78 Firdaws, Jami' Mosque, about 1200. Devastated by the earthquake of 1968, the ivan's facade bears numerous decorative elements, and in the style of Khurasan is opposed by only one other ivan across the courtyard.

Plate 79 Khurramabad Tower, 12th century. This isolated tower may have functioned as a signal-tower as well as for the call to prayer. The unornamented shaft is now about 25 metres high. The base, recently restored, is of stone.

Plate 80 Zuzan, Malik-i Zuzan Mosque, 1219. Built at the end of the Khwarazmshah period, only two damaged ivans are now extant. The sanctuary ivan with the remains of the vaulting just visible is a massive brick-built structure indicative of trends at the time.

Plate 81 Zuzan, Malik-i Zuzan Mosque, 1219. The massive brick structure of the eastern ivan has traces of a great epigraphic frieze as well as developed stalactite vaulting below the missing upper section.

Plate 82 Zuzan, Mosque of
Malik-i Zuzan, ivan detail, 13th
century. The facade of the sanctuary
ivan has a monumental terracotta
inscription overlaying a richly
carved terracotta ground. The
inscription is framed by massive
interlaced guard-bands of unglazed
brick with a carved terracotta infill.
The occasional use of blue glazed
bricks highlights both inscription
and guard-bands.

Plate 83 Farumad, Mosque, probably 13th century. Now in a bad state of repair, this little mosque is of the two-ivan type common in Khurasan. Although it may be dated to the early thirteenth century some of its decorative elements suggest a slightly later date.

Plate 84 Farumad, Mosque, detail, probably 13th century. Many of the arch soffits in the mosque's arcades are decorated with elaborate stucco panels. Many of the elements in the decoration have antecedents in the Saljuq period.

Plate 85 Farumad, Mosque, stucco panel, probably 13th century. Typical of many such panels in the mosque, plaster is incised with various patterns inspired by earlier brick decoration but bearing no relation to the actual brick structure unlike similar ornamentation in the previous period.

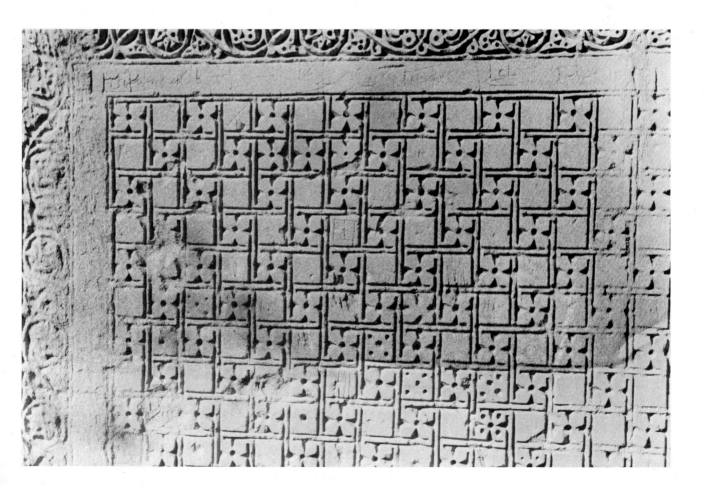

Plates 86 and 87 Hamadan, Gunbad-i 'Alaviyan, Tomb, ? late 13th century. Dates from the twelfth to the fourteenth century have been ascribed to this building. Many features of its decoration have their genesis in the Saljuq period but the rich complexity of the decoration tends to point to a date in the late thirteenth or early fourteenth century.

Plates 88 and 89 Hamadan, Gunbad-i 'Alaviyan, Tomb, details, ? late 13th century. An interesting feature is the wealth of decoration on the exterior as well as the more expected carved stucco on the interior. This exterior decoration is demonstrated by the intricacy of the epigraphic frieze around the door and by the dramatic brick patterns on the side walls.

Plate 90 Sava, Imamzada
Sayyid Ishaq, Tomb, 1277–78. This
structure has suffered from
numerous restorations and is dated
from a glazed inscription frieze now
covering the gravestone inside. The
strangely shaped dome is probably a
later addition.

Plate 91 Sarvistan, Imamzada Shaykh Yusuf, Tomb, 1281–1349. Several inscriptions within the structure provide the dates. The most interesting feature is the use of the massive stone pillars with their stalactite carved capitals and bulbous bases.

Plates 92 and 93 Varamin, 'Ala ad-Din Tomb Tower, 1289. Built during the Mongol period, the exterior is formed of 32 right-angled flanges. Just below the conical roof is an inscription and decorative elements in blue faience. The vertical joints between the bricks forming the flanges are decorated with plaster brick plugs. (Photo: Warwick Ball.)

Plate 94 Tus, Haruniyya Tomb, 13th/14th century. Probably deriving from the twelfth century tomb of Sanjar in Soviet Central Asia, general evidence tends to suggest a date around 1300. The exterior is dominated by the great double dome and the massive exterior wall, whilst the interior is lighter in feeling and has complicated domed ceilings.

Plate 95 Gar, Domed Structure, Mihrab, 13th century. This ruined Mongol dome chamber is adjacent to a much earlier Saljuq minaret dated 1121–22. The much restored mihrab has traces of a very fine stucco decoration while an inscription on the opposite wall would suggest a date around 1290.

Plate 96 Varamin, Imamzada Yahya Mausoleum, 13th century. Dates from 1261 to 1307 are accredited to this tomb. Formerly it contained fine lustre tilework and a lustre faience mihrab. Other buildings forming part of the complex have vanished. The exterior is square with an octagonal chamber supporting the stepped dome on deep squinches.

Plate 97 Varamin, Imamzada Yahya Mausoleum, frieze detail, about 1300.
Although its former lustre ornament is no longer in the shrine, much of the painted
and carved stucco is extant including a deep frieze which surmounted the mihrab.

153

Plates 98 and 99 'Aliabad Kishmar, Tomb Tower, about 1300. The arched portal is set within a deep rectangular frame which cuts into the alternating flanges and half-round columns adorning the twelve-sided exterior. The octagonal interior is divided into deep niches in two storeys by eight piers, one of which contains a spiral staircase.

Plates 100 and 101 Mahallat-i Bala, Imamzada Abu'l-Fadl wa Yahya, Mihrab, 1308. Located within the shrine complex of Abu'l-Fadl wa Yahya, most of which dates from the eighteenth century or later, the mihrab of 1308 has several Qur'anic inscriptions as well as decorative motifs executed in stucco.

Plate 102 Haftshuya, Mosque, early 14th century. This badly ruined Il Khanid mosque is built around the remains of a much earlier structure. Traces of the base of a Saljuq minaret lie adjacent whilst the later dome chamber incorporates a Saljuq mihrab.

Plate 103 Haftshuya, Mosque, early 14th century. The remaining walls of the dome chamber are covered with a layer of stucco on which is incised a brick pattern bearing no relation to the inferior wall construction. The pattern is continued on the soffit of the arch.

Plate 104 Haftshuya, Mosque Mihrab, early 14th century. The mihrab is a good example of contemporary stucco work and is in a fine state of preservation.

Plate 105 Linjan, Pir-i Bakran Mausoleum, early 14th century. The ivan, part of an earlier structure, was the teaching area of a notable divine which upon his death became his mausoleum. A curtain wall was built across the ivan entrance and a mihrab built into the wall; entry was provided by a corridor made in the side of the ivan. Dates of 1303 and 1312 are found in the complex.

Plates 106 and 107 Linjan, Pir-i Bakran Mausoleum, interior, early 14th century. The whole interior of this shrine is richly decorated using deeply carved stucco, incised plaster, terracotta and glazed tiles. In addition to the vegetal scroll-work there are a number of inscription panels in stylised script, whilst the spaces between the bricks are ornamented with carved brick-end plugs. The semi-dome above the central tomb has stalactite vaulting covered with incised plaster decoration.

Plate 108 Linjan, Pir-i Bakran
Mausoleum, early 14th century.
View over the surrounding village
situated not far from Isfahan seen
from one of the openings in the upper
part of the ivan.

Plate 109 Bistam, Shrine of Bayazid, early 14th century. Since the saint's death in the ninth century, his tomb has been a place of pilgrimage and hence of construction. The conical-roofed structure is the central tomb and local tradition ascribes it to Bayazid himself, although it has been much restored.

Plate 110 Bistam, Shrine of
Bayazid, early 14th century. Across
the courtyard from the entrance
stands an ivan with a half-dome with
stalactites; the ivan facade is
decorated with faience.

Plate 111 Bistam, Shrine of Bayazid, detail, early 14th century. The geometric pattern around the facade of the ivan is of shaped brick and originally included faience, traces of which still remain.

Plate 112 Bistam, Jami' Mosque
Mihrab, detail, 1302. Near the
shrine complex is a small mosque
with a tomb tower alongside. The
mosque contains a mihrab which is a
fine example of Mongol stucco. The
intricate patterns and inscriptions are
similar to such contemporary work as
Uljaytu's mihrab in Isfahan.

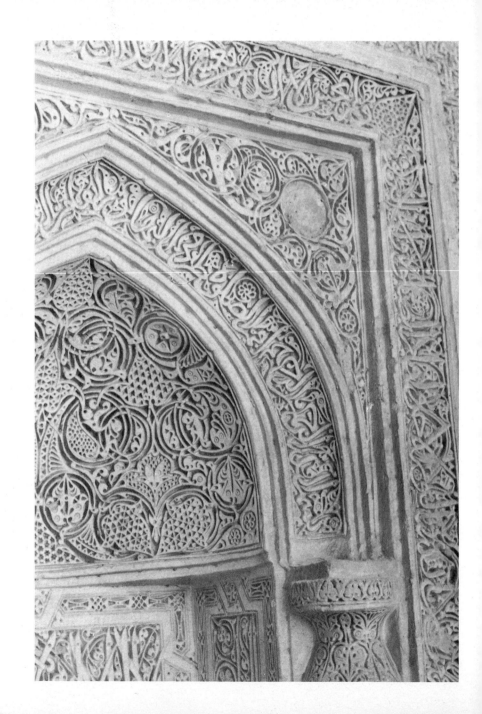

Plate 113 Bistam, Tomb Tower, detail, 1313. This tomb tower with its stellate flanges has delicate inscription panels just below the cornice supporting the roof. The vertical brick joints have decorated plaster plugs.

Plates 114 and 115 Isfahan, Jami' Mosque, Mihrab of Uljaytu, 1310. The mihrab was constructed for the Il Khanid ruler Uljaytu in a prayer hall within the old mosque. It is an outstanding example of Mongol stucco work with intricate inscriptions and patterns. Two wooden minbars (pulpits) flank the mihrab, the righthand one of which is reputed locally to be contemporary with the mihrab.

Plate 116 Sultaniyya, Tomb of
Uljaytu, early 14th century.
Currently undergoing extensive
restoration work, the great domed
mausoleum of Uljaytu, who died in
1317, still dominates the village sited
on the remains of the city he founded.
The structure stands over 50 metres
high and its dome was formerly
covered with blue glazed tiles. At the
base of the dome are eight minarets
springing from the corner angles.
(Photo: Warwick Ball.)

Plate 117 Ashtarjan, Jami' Mosque, about 1315. The domed sanctuary area is preceded by a vaulted ivan. It is likely that the dome chamber was the first element of the mosque and that the adjacent buildings and portal were added shortly after.

Plate 118 Ashtarjan, Jami'
Mosque, side portal detail, about
1315. The frieze above this doorway
bears an inscription over which is the
stalactite vaulting covered by a layer
of plaster; the plaster is incised with
patterns to suggest brickwork.

Plate 119 Ashtarjan, Jami'
Mosque, detail, about 1315. The
main portal of the mosque is
ornamented with tile mosaic patterns
and a dated inscription for 1315 as
well as a series of niches decorated
with shaped terracotta and glazed
bricks.

Plate 120 Natanz, Shrine of 'Abd
as-Samad, 14th century. The
elements in the present complex date
from 1304 with subsequent additions
and restorations; the lofty minaret is
dated 1325. The pyramidal roof is
over the tomb of the Shaykh which is
dated 1307.

Plate 121 Natanz, Shrine of 'Abd as-Samad, Minaret, 1325. The upper section of the minaret which formerly supported balconies has cornices formed by stalactites covered with faience. The shaft is decorated with a series of glazed bricks.

Plate 122 Natanz, Shrine Complex, Side Entrance, 14th century. The simple doorway flanked by niches also has an inscription panel. The vertical joints of the bricks are ornamented with incised plaster plugs.

Plate 123 Sultaniyya, Chelebi Oghlu Tomb, 14th century. This brick-built octagonal tomb surmounted by a cupola probably dates from about 1330. It stands alongside a badly ruined complex dated 1333 near the tomb of Uljaytu. Each side of the tomb has a pointed arch recessed panel; the decoration is formed by the lay of the bricks and brick plugs, and formerly included some use of faience. (Photo: Warwick Ball.)

Plate 124 Varamin, Jami' Mosque, 1322. Built in the four-ivan style, the mosque has recently been restored. The ivan before the domed sanctuary is decorated with brick patterns and glazed brick. The ivan's semi-dome is supported by a series of stalactites. (Photo: Warwick Ball.)

Plate 125 Varamin, Jami' Mosque, squinch, 1322. The poly-lobed squinch refers
back to that of Gulpaygan, the stalactite brick vaulting giving additional complexity.
Below the squinch is a long calligraphic frieze. The stucco mihrab is
extraordinarily richly carved already showing signs of decadence and occupying most
of the end wall of the sanctuary.

Plate 126 Maragha, Ghaffariyya
Tomb Tower, 14th century. One of
the finest of the group surviving at
Maragha, the Ghaffariyya was
probably constructed before 1328.
The main facade is richly decorated
with glazed brick in black, white and
blue. The tomb stands on a dressed
stone socle. An inscription is
contained within the rectangular
panel above the entrance.

Plate 127 Maragha, Ghaffariyya Tomb Tower, detail, 14th century. Glazed and unglazed brick, prominent under the Mongols, was used to create fine geometric patterns and inscriptions. These bricks were specially moulded and set in plaster.

183

Plate 128 Sarakhs, Baba Luqman Mausoleum, mid-14th century. This impressive mausoleum is modelled on the Haruniyya at Tus. The ruins of a high ivan preface the square tomb chamber which is crowned by a double dome. An inscription records a date of 1356.

Plate 129 Sarakhs, Baba Luqman Mausoleum, squinch, mid-14th century. The dome chamber interior is heavily plastered. The deep niches of the lower section with their stalactite semi-domes are sharply divided from the zone of transition to the dome. Unlike earlier Saljuq and Mongol dome chambers which have a feeling of unity, this division seems to recall the much earlier dome chamber at Sangbast.

Plate 130 Isfahan, Dardasht Minarets, 14th century. Now only the domed tomb and the portal crowned by its minarets remain of a larger complex. The dome on its high drum may pre-date the portal. The minarets and dome are decorated with glazed and unglazed bricks.

Plate 131 Gurgan, Imamzada Nur Tomb Tower, probably 14th century. This polygonal tomb with its modern roof is decorated with numerous panels of brick patterns. It is probably Mongol but the brickwork is reminiscent of earlier styles.

Plate 132 and 133 Gurgan, Imamzada Nur Tomb Tower, probably 14th century. The decorative brickwork covering the entire exterior of the monument is both rich and varied. The portal is crowned with a stalactite niche whilst some of the side panels recall patterns on the sides of the 'Alaviyan in Hamadan rather than earlier motifs as found in Damghan. The style therefore justifies the somewhat later dating.

Plate 134 Sunqur Tomb Tower, 14th century. This simple octagonal brick structure is set on a base made of unsquared stone. This technique is a local tradition and is still used in much of the area's vernacular architecture.

Plate 135 Sirjan, Shah Firuz Tomb, detail, 14th century. This unusual domed kiosk tomb is now in a bad state of repair. However part of the inner dome remains showing the rib-vaulting. These ribs were constructed from wood which was then plastered and painted.

191

Plate 136 Kuh-i Banan, Tomb, 14th/15th century. This structure may date from the end of the Il Khan period and its unusual shape has no parallel. From early times the area was associated with religious fraternities, as evidenced by nearby Saljuq remains, and continued as such until the fifteenth century. This building may thus be linked to this tradition.